Betty Crocker
PICTURE COOKBOOK

FRUIT DESSERTS

GOLDEN PRESS/NEW YORK
Western Publishing Company, Inc.
Racine, Wisconsin

Copyright © 1982, 1975 by General Mills, Inc., Minneapolis, Minn.
All rights reserved. Produced in the U.S.A.

Library of Congress Catalog Card Number: 81-83381
ISBN 0-307-09668-8

Golden® and Golden Press® are trademarks of
Western Publishing Company, Inc.

CONTENTS

Cinnamon-Apple Tart	5
Baked Apples Moroccan	6
Apple Whirl	8
Mallow Apples	9
Banana Roll-ups	10
Banana Pops	13
Cherry Bananas	13
Flaming Blueberry Sundaes	14
Fresh Berry Trifle	16
Berry Puddings	17
Christmas Pudding	18
Raspberry Revel Meringue	21
Rum-Berry Angel	22
Two-Berry Whip	22
Berry Crème	23
French Strawberry Torte	24
Cool Treats	24
Summer Shortcakes	27
Berry Shake	28
Berry Shiver	29
Cherry Cream Puff Ring	30
Cherry Tortonis	32
Cherry Frost	32
Honeydew Ice	34
Dixie Cantaloupe and Peaches	35

Melon Parfaits	**37**
Melon Ring	**37**
Orange Freeze	**38**
Orange Custard	**39**
Peach Rosettes	**40**
Baby Blintze Stacks	**42**
Ruby Peaches	**44**
Meringue Pears	**44**
Spiced Pears	**46**
Sherried Pears	**47**
Pineapple Polynesian	**48**
Stained Glass Window Trifle	**51**
Pineapple Shortcake	**52**
Sherry Trifle	**53**
Fruit Wedges	**53**
Peachy Plum Cobbler	**54**
Spicy Pumpkin Squares	**56**
Deluxe Pumpkin Custards	**59**
Sparkling Fruit	**60**
Honey Grapes	**61**
Minted Fruit	**62**
Rum Praline Parfaits	**63**
Fruit-Cheese Tray	**64**

Simmer candy mixture until the candies are partially dissolved; pour into pan. Cook and stir the apples just until crisp-tender.

Arrange apples on cinnamon mixture, placing outer edges down. Place pastry circle on apples. After baking, cool and invert.

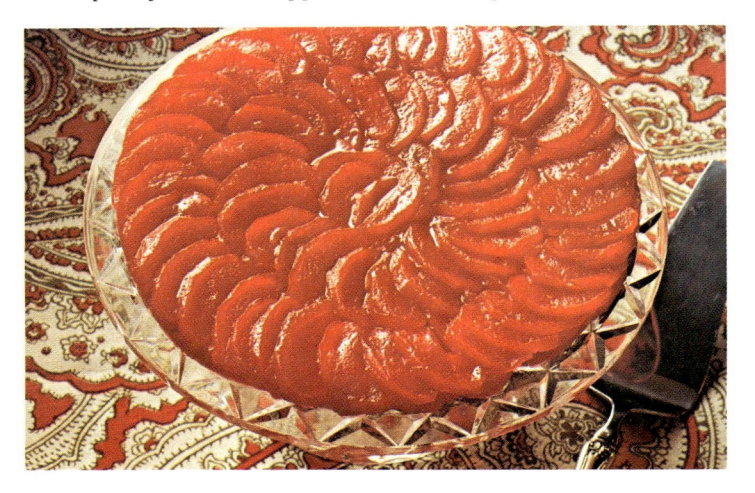

Cinnamon-Apple Tart

- ¾ cup cinnamon candies
- 2 tablespoons water
- 2 tablespoons light corn syrup
- 2 tablespoons packed brown sugar
- 2 tablespoons butter or margarine
- 5 medium apples (such as Rhode Island, Greening or Winesap), pared and thinly sliced (about 5 cups)
- 1 package (11 ounces) pie crust mix or sticks
- ½ cup chilled whipping cream (optional)

Heat cinnamon candies, water and corn syrup to boiling; reduce heat. Simmer uncovered, stirring occasionally, until candies are partially dissolved, about 10 minutes. Pour cinnamon mixture into ungreased round layer pan, 9x1½ inches. Cool.

Heat brown sugar and butter in 10-inch skillet, stirring constantly, until sugar is dissolved. Add apples. Cook and stir until apples are crisp-tender, 3 to 4 minutes. Cool.

Heat oven to 425°. Arrange apples on cinnamon mixture in pan. Prepare pastry for One-Crust Pie as directed on pie crust mix package. Roll pastry into 9-inch circle on floured cloth-covered board. Place pastry circle on apples. Bake until pastry is light golden brown, 40 to 45 minutes.

Cool about 1 hour. Invert on serving plate. Beat whipping cream in chilled small mixer bowl until stiff. Cut tart into wedges; top with whipped cream. 8 TO 10 SERVINGS.

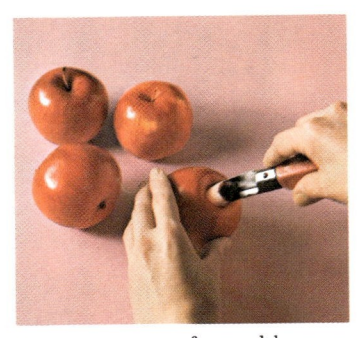

Remove core from blossom end of each apple, leaving about ¼ inch at the stem end.

Pare the upper half of each apple to prevent the peel from splitting while apples bake.

Baked Apples Moroccan

- 6 medium baking apples
- 6 tablespoons cut-up dates or raisins
- 6 tablespoons honey
- Whipped Brandy Sauce (right)

Heat oven to 375°. Remove core from blossom end of each apple, leaving about ¼ inch at stem end. Remove 1-inch strip of peel around middle of each apple or pare upper half as pictured to prevent peel from splitting. Place apples stem ends down in ungreased baking dish, 9x9x2 inches. Spoon about 1 tablespoon dates and 1 tablespoon honey into center of each apple. Pour ¼ inch water into baking dish.

Bake uncovered until apples are tender when pierced with fork, 45 to 50 minutes, spooning syrup in baking dish onto apples several times during baking. (Baking time will vary with size and variety of apples.) Serve warm or cool with Whipped Brandy Sauce.   6 SERVINGS.

WHIPPED BRANDY SAUCE

1 cup chilled whipping cream
¼ cup sugar
1 teaspoon brandy flavoring

Beat whipping cream, sugar and brandy in chilled small mixer bowl until stiff.

Timing Tip: If you want to serve at different times, Baked Apples Moroccan will hold in refrigerator up to 24 hours. Whipped Brandy Sauce will hold in refrigerator up to 8 hours.

APPLES, about 70 calories each, come in 7,000 varieties. Choose firm apples (such as Rome Beauty) for baking, tart (Greenings) for pies, and sweet (Red and Golden Delicious) for munching. One pound (3 medium) generally yields about 3 cups of cut-up apples. Look for firm, blemish-free apples. Keep them cold.

Apple Whirl

- 1 envelope unflavored gelatin
- ¼ cup cold water
- 6 medium apples, cut into fourths
- ⅓ cup packed brown sugar
- 2 tablespoons lemon juice
- Dash of salt
- 1 cup frozen whipped topping, thawed
- ½ cup granola (any flavor)

Sprinkle gelatin on cold water in saucepan to soften; stir over low heat until gelatin is dissolved. Cool.

Place gelatin mixture, ¼ of the apples, the brown sugar, lemon juice and salt in blender container. Cover and blend on high speed until smooth, about 1 minute. Add remaining apples, a few at a time, blending until smooth. Pour mixture into large bowl; fold in whipped topping. Divide among 9 dessert dishes. Refrigerate at least 1 hour; sprinkle with granola.   9 SERVINGS.

Mallow Apples

  6 medium apples, cut into ½-inch slices
  1 can (12 ounces) sugar-free apple-flavored carbonated beverage
½ teaspoon ground cinnamon
¼ teaspoon ground nutmeg
  4 large marshmallows, cut in half

Heat all ingredients except marshmallows to boiling in 10-inch skillet, stirring until apples are coated; reduce heat. Cover and simmer until apples are tender, 10 to 15 minutes; spoon into serving dish. Place marshmallow halves on apples. Cover and let stand 2 to 3 minutes.   6 SERVINGS.

Roll pastry into a rectangle; cut rectangle into 6 squares.

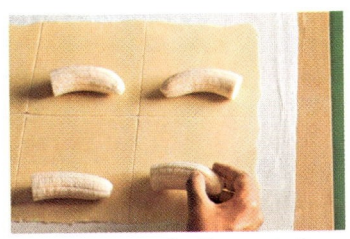

Place banana half 1 inch from end of each square.

Sprinkle brown sugar mixture evenly over banana halves.

Roll up pastry; moisten edges and press to seal securely.

Banana Roll-ups

---

1 package (11 ounces) pie crust sticks
½ cup packed brown sugar
½ teaspoon ground mace
3 medium bananas
Orange Topping (right)

Heat oven to 450°. Prepare 1 pie crust stick as directed on package except—roll pastry into rectangle, 15x10 inches, on floured cloth-covered board. Cut rectangle into 6 squares.

Mix brown sugar and mace. Cut bananas crosswise in half. Place 1 banana half 1 inch from end of each square; sprinkle brown sugar mixture evenly over bananas. Roll up pastry; moisten edges and press to seal. Place on ungreased baking sheet. Bake until golden brown, 10 to 12 minutes. Serve warm with Orange Topping.   6 SERVINGS.

ORANGE TOPPING
- ½ cup chilled whipping cream
- 2 tablespoons packed brown sugar
- ¼ teaspoon orange flavoring
- 1 can (11 ounces) mandarin orange segments, drained

Beat whipping cream, brown sugar and flavoring in chilled small mixer bowl until soft peaks form. Fold in orange segments.

For easy handling, pour mixture into 5-ounce paper cups set in muffin pan.

After freezing until mushy, insert wooden sticks and continue freezing until firm.

Banana Pops

1 envelope (1¼ ounces) low-calorie whipped
   topping mix
1 cup skim milk
⅓ cup orange juice
1 medium banana, mashed
1 tablespoon packed brown sugar
1 teaspoon vanilla
   Grated peel and juice of 1 lemon (about
   1 teaspoon peel and 3 tablespoons juice)

Prepare whipped topping mix as directed on package. Stir in remaining ingredients. Beat on low speed until smooth, about 30 seconds; pour into twelve 5-ounce paper cups or paper-lined medium muffin cups. Freeze until mushy, about 2 hours. Insert wooden sticks and freeze until firm, 5 to 6 hours.   12 POPS.

Cherry Bananas

1 tablespoon butter or margarine
1 tablespoon packed brown sugar
6 medium bananas, cut diagonally into
   chunks
½ cup sugar-free cherry-flavored carbonated
   beverage
¼ cup low-calorie cherry jelly
¼ teaspoon ground cinnamon
1 drop red food color (optional)

Cook and stir butter and brown sugar over medium heat until butter is melted and sugar is dissolved. Add bananas; cook until coated. Remove from heat.

Cook remaining ingredients over low heat, stirring constantly, until jelly is melted; pour sauce on bananas. 8 SERVINGS.

Stir blueberries and lemon juice into the hot sauce.

Heat rum just until warm. Ignite; pour on blueberries.

Flaming Blueberry Sundaes

    Homemade Ice Milk (right)
- ½ cup sugar-free cherry-flavored carbonated beverage
- ¼ cup low-calorie cherry jelly
- 2 cups blueberries
- 1 teaspoon lemon juice
- ¼ cup rum

Prepare Homemade Ice Milk; freeze until firm, at least 8 hours.

Heat carbonated beverage and jelly in 2-quart saucepan, stirring constantly, until jelly is melted and mixture is smooth. Remove from heat. Stir in blueberries and lemon juice; pour into fondue pot.

Heat rum just until warm. Ignite rum and pour on blueberries. Serve over scoops of Homemade Ice Milk.

8 SERVINGS.

HOMEMADE ICE MILK

- 2 teaspoons unflavored gelatin
- 2 tablespoons cold water
- ⅔ cup evaporated skim milk, chilled
- ¼ cup sugar
- 1 teaspoon vanilla

Sprinkle gelatin on cold water in saucepan to soften; stir over low heat until gelatin is dissolved. Beat milk, sugar and vanilla in chilled small mixer bowl on high speed until very thick and fluffy, about 2 minutes. Beat in gelatin gradually until mixture is very stiff, about 3 minutes; pour into ice cube tray.

Fresh Berry Trifle

- 1 package (3¼ ounces) vanilla pudding and pie filling
- 1 teaspoon rum flavoring
- 12 ladyfingers
- 2 cups fresh blueberries or strawberries
- 1 cup chilled whipping cream
- ¼ cup packed brown sugar
- 2 tablespoons toasted sliced almonds

Prepare pudding and pie filling as directed on package for pudding. Cover surface of pudding with plastic wrap to prevent skin from forming. Cool to room temperature; stir in flavoring. Split ladyfingers lengthwise; arrange in 2-quart glass serving bowl, using as many as needed to line bowl. Layer pudding, blueberries and remaining ladyfingers in bowl.

Beat whipping cream and brown sugar in chilled small mixer bowl until stiff. Spread over trifle; sprinkle with almonds. Refrigerate at least 1 hour. To serve, spoon into dessert dishes.   8 TO 10 SERVINGS.

Arrange split ladyfingers in serving bowl, using as many as needed to line bowl.

Layer vanilla pudding, the blueberries and the remaining ladyfingers in bowl.

Berry Puddings

1 can (21 ounces) blueberry pie filling
½ teaspoon ground cinnamon
1 package (16 ounces) frozen blueberries, thawed and drained
2 teaspoons lemon juice
2 packages (3 ounces each) cream cheese, softened
¼ cup powdered sugar
¼ cup chopped nuts

Mix pie filling, cinnamon, blueberries and lemon juice. Spoon into 8 dessert dishes. Beat cheese and sugar in small mixer bowl on medium speed until fluffy; fold in nuts. Spoon topping onto puddings.   8 SERVINGS.

FRESH FRUIT PREPARATION

Here's a tongue twister that makes a lot of sense: When paring apples and pears, pare as thinly as possible. (You don't want to cut away valuable nutrients.)

To loosen the skin of ripe peaches or apricots, first dip them in boiling water for 20 to 30 seconds, then into cold water—the skin will pucker and pull off easily.

Want to avoid a brown-out? You can prevent fruit from discoloring after it has been cut by dipping it in lemon, lime, orange or pineapple juice.

Christmas Pudding

   7 ounces uncooked vermicelli
   2 packages (8 ounces each) cream cheese, softened
   ¾ cup sugar
   3 eggs
   2 teaspoons vanilla
   ¼ teaspoon salt
   1 carton (16 ounces) dairy sour cream
1½ cups golden raisins
   Ground nutmeg
   Cranberry Topping (right)
   Whipped topping

Fold sour cream, vermicelli, raisins into cheese mixture.

To make topping, stir cranberries into thickened juice.

Heat oven to 375°. Cook vermicelli as directed on package; drain. Beat cheese, sugar, eggs, vanilla and salt in large mixer bowl until mixed; fold in sour cream, vermicelli and raisins. Pour into greased baking dish, 13½x8¾x1¾ inches; sprinkle with nutmeg. Bake until brown around edges, about 45 minutes. Serve with Cranberry Topping. Garnish with whipped topping.   12 SERVINGS.

CRANBERRY TOPPING

½ cup sugar
2 tablespoons cornstarch
2 cups cranberry juice cocktail
2 cups cranberries

Mix sugar and cornstarch in 2-quart saucepan. Stir in juice. Cook over medium heat, stirring constantly, until mixture thickens and boils; boil and stir 1 minute. Stir in cranberries; reduce heat. Simmer uncovered until cranberries are tender, about 5 minutes.

Spread half (about 2 cups) of the meringue mixture in 8-inch circle, building up the side.

Drop remaining meringue mixture by rounded teaspoonfuls on edge, making small peaks.

Raspberry Revel Meringue

    Meringue Shell (below)
2 packages (10 ounces each) frozen raspberries, thawed and drained (reserve syrup)
3 tablespoons cornstarch
1 cup chilled whipping cream
1 package (3 ounces) cream cheese, softened
½ cup sugar
½ teaspoon vanilla
1 cup miniature marshmallows

Bake Meringue Shell. Mix ¼ cup of the reserved raspberry syrup and the cornstarch in saucepan. Add raspberries and remaining syrup. Heat to boiling, stirring constantly. Boil and stir 1 minute. Cool to room temperature.

Beat whipping cream in chilled bowl until stiff. Blend cheese, sugar and vanilla. Fold cheese mixture and marshmallows into whipped cream. Spread ⅓ of the raspberry mixture in Meringue Shell. Spread ½ of the cheese mixture over raspberry layer. Repeat, using ½ of the remaining raspberry mixture, the remaining cheese mixture and remaining raspberry mixture. Refrigerate at least 2 hours but no longer than 24 hours.   8 TO 10 SERVINGS.

MERINGUE SHELL

Heat oven to 250°. Cover baking sheet with brown paper. Beat 4 egg whites and ¼ teaspoon cream of tartar in small mixer bowl until foamy. Beat in 1 cup sugar, 1 tablespoon at a time; continue beating until stiff and glossy, about 4 minutes. Spread half of the meringue mixture in 8-inch circle on brown paper, building up side. Drop remaining meringue mixture by rounded teaspoonfuls on edge of circle, making small peaks. Bake 1½ hours. Turn off oven; leave meringue in oven with door closed 1 hour. Remove from oven; cool.

Rum-Berry Angel

2 tablespoons rum or 1 teaspoon rum flavoring
1 cup frozen whipped topping, thawed
1 cup raspberry sherbet, slightly softened
¼ teaspoon almond extract
6 drops green food color
¼ cup slivered almonds
1 cup vanilla ice cream, slightly softened
1 packaged 10-inch angel food cake
2 packages (10 ounces each) frozen raspberries, thawed and drained

Fold rum into ½ cup of the whipped topping; stir into sherbet. Freeze 6 hours.

Fold extract and food color into remaining whipped topping; stir topping mixture and almonds into ice cream. Freeze 6 hours.

Cut 8 to 10 pieces from cake; top each with 1 spoonful of pink and 1 spoonful of green topping. Garnish with raspberries.   8 TO 10 SERVINGS.

Two-Berry Whip

Spoon about ⅓ cup strawberry halves into each of 6 dessert dishes. Mix 1 package (10 ounces) frozen raspberries, thawed (with liquid), and 1 cup whipping cream, whipped; spoon over strawberries.   6 SERVINGS.

THINK CALORIES! The taste and texture of these cheeses are similar, but the calories vary. One ounce of cream cheese amounts to 105 calories. The same amount of Neufchâtel is only 75 calories.

THINK CALORIES! The taste and texture of dairy sour cream and yogurt are similar, but the calories vary. One half cup dairy sour cream comes to 230 calories in contrast to only 65 calories for yogurt.

Berry Crème

---

1 cup boiling water
1 envelope low-calorie raspberry-flavored gelatin
2 tablespoons sugar
1 cup vanilla ice milk
1 carton (8 ounces) unflavored yogurt
3 ounces Neufchâtel cheese, softened
2 teaspoons lemon juice
⅓ cup raspberries

Pour boiling water on gelatin and sugar in large mixer bowl; stir until gelatin and sugar are dissolved. Beat in ice milk, yogurt, cheese and lemon juice until smooth. Divide among 6 dessert dishes; refrigerate no longer than 3 hours. Just before serving, top each dessert with a few raspberries.   6 SERVINGS.

French Strawberry Torte

1¼ cups biscuit baking mix
¼ cup sugar
1 tablespoon grated orange peel
¼ cup butter or margarine, softened
1 pint fresh strawberries, cut in half
½ cup orange juice
¼ cup water
2 tablespoons sugar
1 tablespoon cornstarch
½ cup chilled whipping cream
2 tablespoons sugar

Heat oven to 400°. Mix baking mix, ¼ cup sugar and the orange peel. Cut in butter until mixture resembles coarse cornmeal. Press mixture in ungreased round layer pan, 9x1½ inches. Bake until light brown, 10 to 12 minutes. Cool about 30 minutes.

Invert crust on serving plate. Arrange strawberries on crust. Mix orange juice, water, 2 tablespoons sugar and the cornstarch in saucepan. Heat to boiling, stirring constantly. Boil and stir 1 minute. Cool completely. Pour orange glaze on strawberries. Refrigerate 1 hour.

Beat whipping cream and 2 tablespoons sugar until stiff. Garnish torte with whipped cream. 8 TO 10 SERVINGS.

Cool Treats

For each parfait, layer ⅓ cup sliced strawberries, ½ teaspoon orange-flavored liqueur, 1 spoonful frozen whipped topping, thawed, a few mandarin orange segments, ½ teaspoon orange-flavored liqueur and additional whipped topping in each parfait glass. Repeat if desired. Top with a strawberry.

Cut in butter until mixture resembles coarse cornmeal.

Press mixture in an ungreased round layer pan and bake.

Arrange the strawberry halves on the cooled baked crust.

Pour the orange glaze evenly on the strawberry halves.

Mound softened ice cream, then fruit on the bottom half of each split shortcake.

Top the assembled shortcakes with additional spoonfuls of the sweetened berries.

Summer Shortcakes

  1 pint strawberries, cut in half
  1 pint blueberries
  ¼ cup sugar
  2⅓ cups biscuit baking mix
  3 tablespoons sugar
  ⅔ cup light cream (20%)
    Light cream
    Vanilla ice cream, slightly softened

Heat oven to 450°. Mix strawberries, blueberries and ¼ cup sugar; cover and refrigerate.

Stir baking mix, 3 tablespoons sugar and ⅔ cup cream until a soft dough forms. Gently smooth dough into ball on floured cloth-covered board. Knead 8 to 10 times. Roll dough ½ inch thick. Cut with floured 3-inch round or 4-inch star-shaped cutter or sharp knife; place on ungreased baking sheet. Brush tops with cream. Bake until light brown, about 10 minutes.

Split shortcakes. Mound ice cream on bottom halves. Spoon half of the berry mixture onto ice cream. Top with remaining shortcake halves and berry mixture.

8 SERVINGS.

Berry Shake

- 1 can (12 ounces) sugar-free strawberry-flavored carbonated beverage, chilled
- ¼ cup strawberry ice cream
- 1 medium banana, sliced
- 2 ice cubes
- 2 large strawberries

Place all ingredients except strawberries in blender container. Cover and blend on high speed until well mixed, about 30 seconds. Garnish each shake with 1 strawberry. Serve immediately.   2 SERVINGS.

Berry Shiver

- ½ cup sugar
- ½ cup nonfat dry milk
- 2 teaspoons unflavored gelatin
- ⅔ cup sugar-free strawberry-flavored carbonated beverage
- 1 package (10 ounces) frozen sliced strawberries, partially thawed
- 1 tablespoon lemon juice

Mix sugar, dry milk and gelatin in 2-quart saucepan. Stir in carbonated beverage gradually. Heat until mixture is hot (do not boil); pour into ice cube tray. Freeze uncovered until almost firm, about 45 minutes.

Pour strawberry mixture into chilled small mixer bowl. Beat in strawberries and lemon juice until creamy, 2 to 3 minutes; pour into ice cube tray. Cover and freeze until firm, about 3 hours. Divide among 6 dessert dishes.
6 SERVINGS.

Pour the hot milk-gelatin mixture into ice cube tray; freeze uncovered until almost firm.

Beat berries and juice into frozen mixture; pour into ice cube tray. Freeze until firm.

Cherry Cream Puff Ring

1 cup water
½ cup butter or margarine
1 cup all-purpose flour
4 eggs
1 cup milk
¾ cup dairy sour cream
1 package (3¾ ounces) vanilla instant pudding and pie filling
¼ teaspoon almond extract
1 can (21 ounces) cherry pie filling

Heat oven to 400°. Heat water and butter to boiling in 1-quart saucepan; stir in flour. Stir vigorously until mixture forms a ball, about 1 minute. Remove from heat. Add eggs; beat until smooth. (Or place dough in small mixer bowl; add eggs and beat on low speed 2 minutes.) Drop dough by tablespoonfuls onto greased baking sheet as pictured to form an 8-inch ring (see note). Smooth with spatula. Bake until puffed and golden, 50 to 60 minutes. Cool ring.

Cut off top with sharp knife; pull out any soft dough. Beat milk, sour cream, pudding and pie filling (dry) and extract in small mixer bowl on low speed until blended, about 1 minute. Fill cream puff ring with pudding mixture; spoon ½ cup of the cherry pie filling onto pudding mixture. Replace top of cream puff ring and spoon remaining cherry filling on top. Refrigerate until serving time. 10 TO 12 SERVINGS.

Note: To form ring, place an 8-inch round layer pan on baking sheet and trace around it; drop dough inside circle.

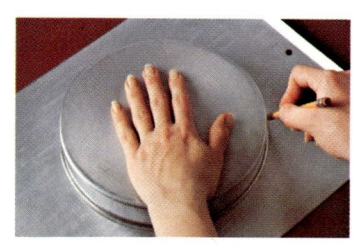

To form ring, place an 8-inch round layer pan on baking sheet and trace around it.

Stir flour mixture vigorously until it leaves the side of saucepan and forms a ball.

Drop dough by tablespoonfuls inside the traced circle to form 8-inch cream puff ring.

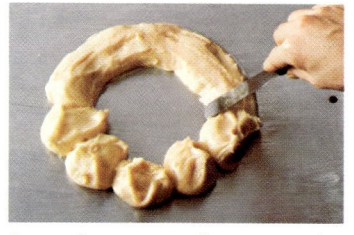

Smooth ring with a spatula, then bake until puffed and golden, 50 to 60 minutes.

Cherry Tortonis

⅔ cup crushed granola (any flavor)
20 large maraschino cherries, finely chopped (about ⅓ cup)
1 teaspoon almond extract
Dash of salt
1 carton (9 ounces) frozen whipped topping, thawed
3 maraschino cherries, cut into fourths

Fold ½ cup of the granola, the chopped cherries, extract and salt into whipped topping. Divide among 12 small baking cups. Freeze uncovered until firm, about 2 hours. Sprinkle tortonis with remaining granola; garnish with cherries. 12 SERVINGS.

Cherry Frost

1 cup boiling water
¾ cup sugar
1 envelope low-calorie cherry-flavored gelatin
1 quart skim milk
Grated peel and juice of 1 lemon (about 1 teaspoon peel and 3 tablespoons juice)
2½ cups pitted dark sweet cherries

Pour boiling water on sugar and gelatin in 2-quart bowl; stir until sugar and gelatin are dissolved. Stir in milk, lemon peel and juice; pour into ice cube trays. Freeze uncovered until firm around edges, about 45 minutes.

Beat milk mixture in chilled large mixer bowl until creamy, about 2 minutes; pour into ice cube trays. Cover and freeze until firm, 5 to 6 hours. Divide among 10 dessert dishes. Top each serving with ¼ cup of the cherries.   10 SERVINGS.

Fold ½ cup granola, the cherries, almond extract and salt into the whipped topping.

Divide the mixture among 12 small aluminum foil baking cups; freeze uncovered.

Honeydew Ice

- 1 medium honeydew melon
- ⅓ cup honey
- ¼ cup lime juice
- ⅛ teaspoon salt
- Ginger ale (optional)

Cut melon in half; remove seeds. Pare and cut melon into 1-inch pieces. Place 1 cup of the melon pieces, the honey, lime juice and salt in blender container. Cover and blend until smooth, 1 to 2 minutes. Add remaining melon pieces; blend until smooth. Pour into 2 ice cube trays; freeze until mushy, about 1 hour.

Pour melon mixture into chilled large mixer bowl; beat on low speed until fluffy, about 2 minutes. Turn into ice cube trays and freeze until firm, at least 4 hours. Serve in dessert dishes or place scoops of ice in tall glasses; fill glasses with ginger ale. 4 TO 6 SERVINGS.

Cantaloupe Ice: Substitute 1 medium cantaloupe for the honeydew melon. Substitute ⅓ cup corn syrup for the honey and 2 tablespoons lemon juice for the lime juice.

Dixie Cantaloupe and Peaches

1 medium cantaloupe, pared and cut into ½-inch pieces (about 3 cups)
4 fresh peaches, peeled and sliced (about 3 cups)
2 tablespoons lemon juice
1 cup all-purpose flour*
1 cup packed brown sugar
⅓ cup butter or margarine
½ teaspoon ground cinnamon
⅛ teaspoon salt
Ice cream or light cream (optional)

Heat oven to 375°. Place cantaloupe and peaches in ungreased baking dish, 8x8x2 inches, or 1½-quart casserole; sprinkle with lemon juice. Mix remaining ingredients except ice cream with pastry blender or fork until crumbly; sprinkle over cantaloupe and peaches. Bake until cantaloupe and peaches are tender and topping is golden brown, about 30 minutes. Serve warm with ice cream.
6 SERVINGS.

*If using self-rising flour, omit salt.

Stir water and wine into the gelatin mixture; refrigerate.

Mix the fruit for parfaits; cover. Refrigerate 1 hour.

Beat the chilled gelatin mixture with a fork until frothy.

Layer the gelatin and fruit in each of 6 parfait glasses.

Melon Parfaits

1 cup boiling water
1 envelope low-calorie lime-flavored gelatin
⅓ cup cold water
⅓ cup sweet white wine (sauterne or Tokay)
½ medium honeydew melon or cantaloupe, cut into balls (about 2 cups)
½ medium pineapple, cut into cubes (about 2 cups)
1 medium orange, sectioned and membrane removed
1 cup strawberries, cut in half

Pour boiling water on gelatin in bowl; stir until gelatin is dissolved. Stir in cold water and wine. Pour into baking pan, 8x8x2 inches. Refrigerate until firm, about 2 hours.

Mix melon balls, pineapple cubes, orange sections and strawberry halves. Cover and refrigerate at least 1 hour. Beat gelatin with fork until frothy. Layer gelatin and fruit in 6 parfait glasses.   6 SERVINGS.

Melon Ring

1 slice watermelon, 1½ inches thick
1 can (11 ounces) mandarin orange segments, chilled and drained
1 medium apple, cored and thinly sliced
Mint leaves

Cut melon from watermelon slice, leaving 1-inch rim. Cut melon into bite-size pieces; remove seeds. Place melon ring on serving plate. Mix melon pieces, orange segments and apple slices. Mound fruit in melon ring and on plate around ring. Garnish with mint leaves.   6 SERVINGS.

Orange Freeze

1¼ cups orange juice
⅓ cup sugar
¼ cup lemon juice
1 carton (4½ ounces) frozen whipped
   topping, thawed
3 tablespoons granola (any flavor)

Mix orange juice, sugar and lemon juice until sugar is dissolved; pour into ice cube tray. Spread whipped topping over orange juice mixture; sprinkle with granola. Freeze uncovered until firm, 5 to 6 hours. Let stand 10 minutes before serving. Divide among 6 dessert dishes.
6 SERVINGS.

Orange Custard

   3 eggs, slightly beaten
   3 tablespoons sugar
   2 teaspoons grated orange peel
   ½ teaspoon lemon extract
   ½ teaspoon vanilla
   Dash of salt
2½ cups skim milk, scalded
   1 medium orange, peeled and cut into
     6 slices

Heat oven to 350°. Mix eggs, sugar, orange peel, lemon extract, vanilla and salt. Stir in milk gradually. Place orange slice in each of six 6-ounce custard cups; pour custard into cups. Place cups in baking pan, 13x9x2 inches. Pour very hot water into pan to within ½ inch of tops of cups.

Bake until knife inserted in centers comes out clean, about 55 minutes. Remove cups from water. Refrigerate until chilled.   6 SERVINGS.

Place an orange slice in each custard cup; add custard. Place cups in baking pan.

Pour very hot water into pan to within ½ inch of tops. Bake the custards 55 minutes.

Dip hot rosette iron in batter just to top edge, being careful not to go over top.

Fry rosette until golden brown; immediately remove and invert on paper towel.

Peach Rosettes

    Vegetable oil
1 egg
1 tablespoon sugar
½ teaspoon salt
½ cup all-purpose flour*
½ cup water or milk
1 tablespoon vegetable oil
⅓ cup sugar
½ teaspoon ground cinnamon
9 peaches, sliced
¼ cup sugar
    Coffee Whipped Cream (right)

Heat oil (2 to 3 inches) to 400° in small deep saucepan. Beat egg, 1 tablespoon sugar and the salt in small deep bowl. Beat in flour, water and 1 tablespoon oil until smooth.

Heat rosette iron by placing in hot oil 1 minute. Tap excess oil from iron; dip hot iron in batter just to top edge, being careful not to go over top. Fry until golden brown, about 30 seconds. Immediately remove rosette, using fork if necessary; invert on paper towel to cool. (If rosette is not crisp, batter is too thick. Stir in small amount of water or milk.) Heat iron in hot oil before making each rosette. (If iron is not heated, batter will not stick to iron.)

Mix ⅓ cup sugar and the cinnamon. Dip rosettes in sugar mixture. Mix peaches and ¼ cup sugar. Serve rosettes with sweetened peaches and Coffee Whipped Cream.
18 ROSETTES.

*If using self-rising flour, omit salt.

COFFEE WHIPPED CREAM
Beat 1 cup chilled whipping cream, ¼ cup powdered sugar, 1 teaspoon instant coffee, ½ teaspoon vanilla and ⅛ teaspoon ground cardamom or ground cinnamon in chilled small mixer bowl.

Baby Blintze Stacks

Peach Filling (right)
1½ cups all-purpose flour*
1 tablespoon granulated sugar
½ teaspoon baking powder
½ teaspoon salt
½ teaspoon ground nutmeg
2 cups milk
2 eggs
2 tablespoons butter or margarine, melted
½ teaspoon vanilla
½ cup dairy sour cream
2 tablespoons packed brown sugar
Peach slices

Prepare Peach Filling; refrigerate. Mix flour, granulated sugar, baking powder, salt and nutmeg in large bowl. Beat in milk, eggs, butter and vanilla.

Lightly butter griddle; heat until bubbly. Pour batter onto griddle; bake only on 1 side until bottoms are brown. Place blintzes on towel; cover.

For each serving, stack 5 blintzes, spreading 1 tablespoon Peach Filling between each blintze. Mix sour cream and brown sugar; spoon onto blintze stacks. Garnish with peach slices.   10 SERVINGS.

*If using self-rising flour, omit baking powder and salt.

PEACH FILLING
- 1 carton (24 ounces) creamed cottage cheese
- 2 medium peaches, peeled and chopped
- 3 tablespoons sugar
- ½ teaspoon ground nutmeg
- ¼ teaspoon salt
- ¼ teaspoon almond extract

Mix all ingredients thoroughly.

PEACHES are generally divided into 2 types—Clingstone (flesh clings to the pit) and Freestone (flesh separates readily from the pit). Clingstone Elbertas (left) are old home and commercial canning favorites, but many new varieties are popular. Freestones such as Redskins (right) are usually preferred for easy eating.

Ruby Peaches

    6 canned peach halves
    1 cup sugar-free strawberry-flavored
      carbonated beverage
    ¼ cup low-calorie raspberry preserves
    1 tablespoon cornstarch
    6 tablespoons low-calorie whipped topping

Place 1 peach half cut side up in each of 6 dessert dishes. Heat remaining ingredients except topping to boiling, stirring constantly. Boil and stir 1 minute. Cool; top each peach half with 1 tablespoon whipped topping. Pour sauce on peach halves. Refrigerate 2 hours.   6 SERVINGS.

Meringue Pears

     6 medium pears, pared
     ½ cup sugar-free strawberry-flavored
       carbonated beverage
     3 egg whites
     ¼ teaspoon cream of tartar
     ¼ cup powdered sugar
     2 teaspoons grated lemon peel
    12 teaspoons low-calorie strawberry-flavored
       syrup

Heat oven to 350°. Cut pears lengthwise in half; place cut sides down in ungreased baking dish, 11¾x7½x1¾ inches. Pour beverage on pears. Bake uncovered 25 minutes.

Beat egg whites and cream of tartar in small mixer bowl until foamy. Beat in sugar and lemon peel; beat until stiff and glossy. Spoon meringue around pears; pour 1 teaspoon syrup on each. Reduce oven temperature to 300°. Bake until light brown, 16 minutes.   12 SERVINGS.

Pour the strawberry beverage around the pears; bake in a 350° oven.

Spoon the meringue around the pears. Add the syrup; bake in a 300° oven.

Cut pears lengthwise in half; insert cloves in halves.

Simmer pears in orange syrup, turning occasionally.

Spiced Pears

---

　3 large pears, pared
12 whole cloves
　½ cup sugar
　⅔ cup orange juice
　2 tablespoons lemon juice
　1 stick cinnamon
　1 large orange, peeled and thinly sliced
　1 cup seedless green grapes

Cut pears lengthwise in half; insert 2 cloves in broad end of each pear half. Heat sugar, orange juice, lemon juice and cinnamon stick to boiling in 3-quart saucepan, stirring until sugar is dissolved; place pears in orange syrup. Simmer uncovered, turning occasionally, until tender, 10 to 15 minutes. Remove pears to serving dish; add orange slices and grapes. Pour orange syrup on fruit.　　6 SERVINGS.

Sherried Pears

1 can (16 ounces) pear halves, drained
⅓ cup cream sherry
1 can (5 ounces) vanilla pudding (about ½ cup)
Chocolate curls (see note)

Heat pears and sherry to boiling in 8-inch skillet over medium heat, turning pears until coated with sherry. Boil 1 minute; remove from heat.

Place pears cut sides up in 5 dessert dishes; spoon sherry onto pears. Top each pear with generous tablespoon pudding. Garnish with chocolate curls. 5 SERVINGS.

Note: To make chocolate curls, slice across block of semisweet or unsweetened chocolate with vegetable parer or sharp thin knife in long, thin strokes.

PEARS are shipped green; the flavor is finer when ripened off the tree. Bartlett pears (pictured) are popular for commercial and home canning. Don't let a minor blemish on a pear bother you; many kinds have a russeted skin. Cook or bake hard pears or ripen them at room temperature until they are slightly soft for eating.

Ahead of time, shape the ice cream into balls; roll balls in the coconut and freeze.

At the table, stir pineapple into the brown sugar mixture and heat until fruit is hot.

Pineapple Polynesian

1 quart vanilla ice cream
1½ cups flaked coconut
⅔ cup packed brown sugar
1 tablespoon cornstarch
½ cup butter or margarine
1 tablespoon lemon juice
2 teaspoons finely shredded orange peel
4 cups cut-up fresh pineapple (about 1 medium)
¼ cup rum or apricot brandy

Shape ice cream into 6 to 8 balls as pictured and roll in coconut. Place on waxed paper-covered baking sheet and freeze.

Mix brown sugar and cornstarch in chafing dish or skillet; add butter, lemon juice and orange peel. Cook over medium heat, stirring constantly, until mixture thickens and boils. Boil and stir 1 minute. Stir in pineapple; heat until fruit is hot, about 2 minutes. Heat rum in small saucepan just until warm; ignite and pour flaming rum on pineapple. Stir; spoon over each serving of ice cream.
6 TO 8 SERVINGS.

Fresh Fruit Polynesian: Omit coconut. Substitute 4 cups cut-up or sliced fresh fruit for the pineapple. Choose from the following: strawberries and peaches, bananas and raspberries or pears and blueberries.

Cut chilled red and orange gelatins into ¾-inch squares.

Place the ladyfinger halves in baking dish; add half the juice.

Top with half the topping and half of the gelatin squares.

Add ladyfinger halves, juice, fruit, topping and squares.

Stained Glass Window Trifle

1 envelope low-calorie strawberry-flavored gelatin*
1 envelope low-calorie orange-flavored gelatin*
1 package (3 ounces) ladyfingers
1 can (8 ounces) crushed pineapple in juice, drained (reserve juice)
1 envelope (about 2 ounces) whipped topping mix
2 teaspoons sherry flavoring
Dash of salt

Prepare each envelope gelatin separately as directed except—reduce cold water by ¼ cup and pour each about ½ inch deep into baking pan, 8x8x2 inches. Refrigerate until firm, about 3 hours.

Cut gelatins into ¾-inch squares. Place 10 ladyfinger halves in baking dish, 8x8x2 inches; drizzle with half of the reserved pineapple juice. Prepare topping mix as directed on package except—substitute skim milk for the milk and beat in flavoring and salt.

Layer half of the topping and half of the gelatin squares on ladyfinger halves. Top with remaining ladyfinger halves and drizzle with remaining pineapple juice. Top with pineapple. Layer remaining topping and gelatin squares on pineapple. Refrigerate 3 hours.   10 SERVINGS.

*Low-calorie lime- and lemon-flavored gelatins can be substituted for the strawberry- and orange-flavored gelatins.

Pineapple Shortcake

2⅓ cups biscuit baking mix
½ cup milk
3 tablespoons sugar
3 tablespoons butter or margarine, melted
½ teaspoon ground nutmeg
1 can (20 ounces) pineapple slices, drained
⅓ cup sugar*
9 large maraschino cherries
½ cup chopped nuts
1 envelope (about 2 ounces) whipped topping mix

Heat oven to 400°. Grease baking sheet. Stir baking mix, milk, 3 tablespoons sugar, the butter and nutmeg until a soft dough forms. Turn dough onto baking sheet. Pat dough into rectangle, 12x9 inches, with floured hands. (Dough will be sticky.)

Cut 1 pineapple slice into 4 pieces. Dip pieces and remaining slices in ⅓ cup sugar. Press pineapple and cherries into shortcake dough. Sprinkle with nuts. Bake until light brown, about 20 minutes.

Prepare whipped topping as directed on package. Cut shortcake into rectangles. Top each rectangle with whipped topping.   9 SERVINGS.

*1 package (3 ounces) lemon- or lime-flavored gelatin can be substituted for ⅓ cup sugar.

Sherry Trifle

- 2 tablespoons cream sherry
- 9 macaroons, crumbled (about 3½ cups)
- 1 package (3¾ ounces) vanilla instant pudding and pie filling
- 1 can (13¼ ounces) crushed pineapple, well drained
- 1 cup frozen whipped topping, thawed
- ¾ cup chopped nuts

Sprinkle sherry over macaroons; mix thoroughly. Cover and refrigerate 1 hour. Prepare pudding as directed on package. Divide macaroon mixture among 8 dessert dishes. Layer pudding and pineapple over macaroons. Refrigerate until chilled, about 2 hours. Garnish with whipped topping and chopped nuts.   8 SERVINGS.

Fruit Wedges

Mound 1 to 2 tablespoons packed brown sugar in center of each of 6 small plates. Cut top from 1 small pineapple. Cut pineapple into 6 slices; remove core. Cut each slice into wedges and arrange around brown sugar on plates.

Cut 2 oranges into 4 slices each. Cut slices into wedges and arrange on pineapple. Top each serving with a strawberry. Fruit can be dipped in the brown sugar.   6 SERVINGS.

To peel peaches, dip into boiling water 20 to 30 seconds, then into cold water.

The peach skins will loosen and can be pulled off easily with a paring knife.

Peachy Plum Cobbler

1 cup sugar
3 tablespoons cornstarch
½ teaspoon ground cinnamon
3 cups sliced fresh red plums (about 10 to 12 large)
4 medium peaches or nectarines, peeled and sliced (about 3 cups)
1 cup all-purpose flour*
⅓ cup shortening
2 tablespoons sugar
1½ teaspoons baking powder
½ teaspoon salt
¼ cup milk
1 egg, slightly beaten
1 tablespoon sugar
Ice cream or light cream (optional)

Heat oven to 375°. Mix 1 cup sugar, the cornstarch and cinnamon in 3-quart saucepan. Stir in plums and peaches. Cook, stirring constantly, until mixture thickens and boils. Boil and stir 1 minute. Pour into ungreased baking dish, 8x8x2 inches, or 1½-quart casserole.

Mix flour, shortening, 2 tablespoons sugar, the baking powder and salt with pastry blender or fork until crumbly. Stir in milk and egg. Drop dough by spoonfuls onto hot fruit mixture; sprinkle with 1 tablespoon sugar. Bake until topping is golden brown, 25 to 30 minutes. Serve warm with ice cream.   9 SERVINGS.

*If using self-rising flour, omit baking powder and salt.

Spicy Pumpkin Squares

   Graham Cracker Nut Crust (below)
1 can (15 ounces) pumpkin
1 can (13 ounces) evaporated milk
¾ cup sugar
2 eggs
1¾ teaspoons pumpkin pie spice*
1½ cups whipped topping
¾ cup miniature marshmallows
1 teaspoon grated orange peel

Heat oven to 350°. Prepare Graham Cracker Nut Crust. Beat pumpkin, milk, sugar, eggs and pumpkin pie spice until blended; pour into crust. Bake until knife inserted near center comes out clean, about 1 hour. Cool.

Mix whipped topping, marshmallows and orange peel; spread over filling. Refrigerate until serving time.
9 SERVINGS.

*1 teaspoon ground cinnamon, ½ teaspoon ground ginger and ¼ teaspoon ground cloves can be substituted for the pumpkin pie spice.

GRAHAM CRACKER NUT CRUST
½ cup graham cracker crumbs
¼ cup chopped nuts
¼ cup butter or margarine, softened
2 tablespoons sugar

Mix all ingredients; press in ungreased baking pan, 9x9x2 inches. Bake 15 minutes. Cool.

Press graham cracker crust in an ungreased baking pan.

Pour filling into crust; bake and cool. Spread with topping.

After filling the custard cups, carefully place them in a 13x9x2-inch baking pan.

To prevent spilling, pour hot water into the pan after placing it on the oven rack.

Deluxe Pumpkin Custards

2 eggs
1 can (16 ounces) pumpkin
1 cup light cream (20%)
¾ cup packed brown sugar
1 teaspoon pumpkin pie spice
½ teaspoon salt
   Crunchy Pecan Topping (below)
⅛ teaspoon rum flavoring
¼ cup frozen whipped topping, thawed

Heat oven to 350°. Beat eggs, pumpkin, cream, brown sugar, pumpkin pie spice and salt until smooth. Pour into six 6-ounce custard cups. Place cups in baking pan, 13x9x2 inches; pour very hot water into pan to within ½ inch of tops of cups. Bake 20 minutes.

Prepare Crunchy Pecan Topping; sprinkle over custards. Bake until knife inserted halfway between center and edge comes out clean, 30 to 40 minutes. Remove custards from hot water immediately after baking. Just before serving, stir rum flavoring into whipped topping; serve over pecan-topped custards.   6 SERVINGS.

CRUNCHY PECAN TOPPING
Mix ¼ cup chopped pecans, ¼ cup packed brown sugar and 1 tablespoon butter or margarine, softened.

Timing Tip: If you want to serve at different times, Deluxe Pumpkin Custards can be served warm or cold. They will hold in refrigerator up to 48 hours.

Mound the fruit attractively in a pretty compote.

Pour thickened gelatin-wine mixture on fruit.

Sparkling Fruit

- ¾ cup boiling water
- 1 package (3 ounces) peach- or orange-flavored gelatin
- 1¼ cups sweet white wine (sauterne, muscatel, Tokay)
- 1 medium banana, sliced
- 4 medium peaches, cut into eighths
- 1 pint strawberries or raspberries
- 1½ cups seedless green grapes
- Whipped topping
- Ground nutmeg

Pour boiling water on gelatin in bowl; stir until gelatin is dissolved. Stir in wine. Refrigerate until slightly thickened, about 1¼ hours.

Mound fruit in attractive arrangement in compote, shallow glass bowl or 9-inch pie plate. Pour gelatin mixture on fruit. Refrigerate until chilled. Spoon ring of whipped topping around edge; sprinkle topping with nutmeg. 8 SERVINGS.

Honey Grapes

1 pound seedless green grapes
¼ cup honey
3 tablespoons rum
3 small cantaloupes, chilled
½ cup dairy sour cream

Remove stems from grapes. Mix honey and rum; toss with grapes. Refrigerate 2 hours, stirring occasionally.

Cut cantaloupes lengthwise in half, using scalloped cut. Scoop out seeds. Toss grapes with sour cream; spoon into cantaloupes. Drizzle with remaining honey-rum mixture. 6 SERVINGS.

MINT, a versatile herb with a cool, refreshing flavor and fragrance, is often used to flavor fruit cups, salads, desserts and beverages. It is a classic seasoning for lamb, and the snipped fresh or dried leaves are a popular garnish for cooked vegetables and for salads. ½ teaspoon dried mint leaves equals 1 tablespoon fresh.

Minted Fruit

⅓ cup water
¼ cup sugar
1 tablespoon coarsely chopped mint
2 tablespoons orange, pineapple or grapefruit juice
2 cups pineapple spears, strawberries, apple wedges, pear slices, blueberries or melon balls
Lettuce leaves (optional)
Mint leaves

Heat water and sugar to boiling, stirring occasionally; reduce heat. Cover and simmer 5 minutes. Pour on chopped mint; refrigerate 1 hour. Strain; stir in orange juice. Pour mint sauce on fruit. To serve as salad, spoon fruit and mint sauce onto lettuce leaves; garnish with mint leaves.   4 SERVINGS.

Rum Praline Parfaits

- 1 package (3¼ ounces) vanilla pudding and pie filling
- 1 cup light cream (20%)
- ¾ to 1 teaspoon rum flavoring
- 1 tablespoon butter or margarine, softened
- ⅓ cup packed brown sugar
- 2½ to 3 cups fruit (blueberries, strawberries, peaches or grapes)

Prepare pudding and pie filling as directed on package for pudding except—reduce milk to 1¼ cups and add cream. Stir rum flavoring into pudding; cool as directed.

Spread butter on baking sheet, leaving 1½-inch margin on all sides. Sprinkle brown sugar over buttered area. Set oven control to broil and/or 550°. Broil sugar 3 to 4 inches from heat 1 to 2 minutes. (Watch closely—mixture burns easily.) Cool 2 to 3 minutes; remove with spatula and break into pieces. Alternate layers of fruit, rum custard sauce and praline crunch in 8 parfait glasses.   8 SERVINGS.

Timing Tip: If you want to serve at different times, Rum Praline Parfaits will hold in refrigerator up to 2 hours.

Sprinkle brown sugar over the buttered baking sheet.

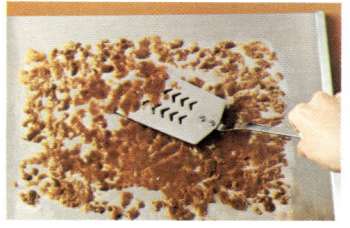

Remove broiled and cooled praline crunch with spatula.

For 1 serving, choose 1 wedge Swiss cheese, ⅓ cantaloupe, ¼ cup grapes and ¼ apple.

Or choose ½ cup grapes, 1 wedge Swiss cheese, ⅔ slice Neufchâtel and ¼ apple.

Or try 2 slices Neufchâtel cheese, ½ cantaloupe and ¼ cup red or green grapes.

Two apple quarters, 1 cup red or green grapes and ⅛ cantaloupe also equal 1 serving.

Fruit-Cheese Tray

- 1 medium cantaloupe, pared and cut into 16 wedges
- 2 medium red apples, cut into fourths
- 8 clusters Tokay or green grapes
- 4 ounces Swiss cheese, cut into 8 wedges
- 3 ounces Neufchâtel cheese, cut into 8 slices
  Salad greens

Arrange fruit and cheese on salad greens.   8 SERVINGS.